Carisbrooke Castle

Christopher Young

Introduction

Carisbrooke Castle has always been the most important stronghold on the Isle of Wight, thanks to its superb defensive position. It crowns a hilltop with commanding views, at the point where the river Medina cuts into the east–west chalk ridge that forms the backbone of the island. Because of the island's location it has also been of great significance in the defence of the realm.

A Norman motte-and-bailey castle was built here in about 1100, succeeding a castle built soon after the Norman invasion of 1066, which in turn was constructed within a late Saxon enclosure. The motte (mound) was an ultimate place of refuge, while the bailey (enclosure) provided space for the headquarters of a great feudal magnate. These huge earthworks demonstrated the newly acquired power and prestige of their builder, Richard de Redvers, who was made lord of the Isle of Wight by Henry I (1100–35). For nearly 200 years the castle was held by the de Redvers family, reverting to the Crown only when the last of them, Countess Isabella de Fortibus, died in 1293.

Over the centuries the castle was adapted to meet new defensive needs, as southern England faced the threat of French and then Spanish invasion; in the 1590s Carisbrooke was one of the few places in England to be wholly refortified as an artillery fortress, with a perimeter over a mile long.

The castle was not only used for defence. It has been the residence of a great lord, a garrison and also a prison – most famously for King Charles I in 1647–8, before his execution. After the Civil War, although it retained a military function, Carisbrooke came to have more of a ceremonial role as a residence of the island's governors, including Princess Beatrice, daughter of Queen Victoria, who used it until 1938. It is still a ceremonial centre for the Isle of Wight, with its chapel acting as the island's war memorial, as well as a tourist attraction.

Above: Detail from the bust of Charles I, attributed to Gian Lorenzo Bernini (1598–1680), in the chapel of St Nicholas

Facing page: The interior of the castle seen from the wall-walk, looking towards the great hall with the keep beyond

Tour

The hilltop at Carisbrooke has been fortified for about a thousand years, underlining its importance as the central stronghold of the Isle of Wight, which lies astride one of the main invasion routes into southern England.

The site is dominated by the massive banks of the Norman motte-and-bailey castle and by the ramparts and bastions of the vast Elizabethan artillery fortress, added in the face of the threat of Spanish invasion. Traces of the late Saxon fort, built to protect the island against Viking raids, are also visible. Within the defences, the various buildings of the castle, frequently adapted to meet changing needs, provide a glimpse of how the castle was used over the centuries by many different owners and residents.

FOLLOWING THE TOUR

The tour takes in the gatehouse, the keep on the motte in the far corner, and the buildings of the inner bailey, before exploring the outer defences. The numbers beside the headings correspond with the small numbered plans in the margins.

Left: The gatehouse. The 14th-century drum towers were cylindrical because corners were more vulnerable to undermining and missiles. The inverted key shapes are loopholes for handguns
Below: Detail of the massive medieval wooden gates at the inner end of the gate-passage

Facing page: The steps leading up the side of the motte to the 12th-century keep

▮ GATEHOUSE
Exterior

The principal entry to the castle for the last 900 years has been through this gateway. Potentially vulnerable to attack, medieval gatehouses were often strongly fortified, and Carisbrooke's was no exception. Flanked by the bank and ditch of the castle built about 1100, the first gatehouse would have been of timber. By 1136 it had been replaced by a stone gatehouse consisting of a tower over the gate-passage, fronted by a deep ditch, which was crossed by a drawbridge. This gatehouse was itself replaced in the late 13th century, probably by Countess Isabella de Fortibus (see page 28) after 1272. It had a rectangular stone tower which still survives. The two cylindrical drum towers were added in 1335–6 in response to the threat of French raids. Projecting towers such as these

provided additional flanking defence for the gate itself. The towers had cross-shaped slits for archers.

Both towers were heightened in 1380, presumably as a reaction to the siege of Carisbrooke by the French in 1377 (see page 29). The new upper stages have gun ports, shaped like inverted keyholes, for the use of early handguns or small artillery pieces on wooden sleds. They were further modified in 1470 when the projecting platform with machicolations – holes through which defenders could drop missiles on enemies attacking the gate below – was added between them. Carved on the parapet, but now very eroded, are the arms of Anthony Woodville, brother-in-law of Edward IV and captain of the island from 1467 to 1483: presumably he ordered the work to be carried out to improve the defences of the gatehouse.

Second floor

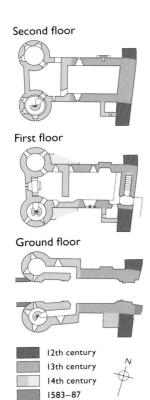

First floor

Ground floor

- 12th century
- 13th century
- 14th century
- 1583–87
- 18th century

N

0   5m   0   15ft

Above: Floor plans of the gatehouse

Below: This early 14th-century manuscript illustration depicts an attack on a gatehouse, which has drum towers similar to those at Carisbrooke

By the late 19th century the gatehouse was roofless and ruinous. It was restored in 1897 by Percy Stone, an architect and local historian who wrote the first modern history of the castle, as a memorial to Prince Henry of Battenberg (1858–96), governor of the Isle of Wight and husband of Princess Beatrice, Queen Victoria's youngest daughter. Stone replaced its roof and some of its floors. The outer gate arch and gates are also part of his restoration.

Gate-Passage

Beneath the cobbles of the gate-passage, excavations uncovered the remains of three drawbridge pits belonging to successive phases of the gate. These pits would have housed the counter-weights of pivoting drawbridges when they were raised. The doorways on either side lead to the two drum towers. The gate-passage contains three portcullis slots, not all of which were in use at the same time. The gates at the inner end of the passage date from the 15th century. They were removed in 1965 to allow entry for Elizabeth II's car when Earl Mountbatten was installed as governor of the island, and have only recently been conserved and replaced.

Interior

Beyond the passage, a stone staircase leads to a small lobby on the first floor. One doorway gives onto a further flight of stairs which originally led to the second floor, now missing, while the other

leads into the main room on the first floor. This was equipped with a fireplace in its north wall. Behind the modern door is the entrance to a small turret which provided a garderobe (lavatory). The second floor was not replaced in the 1897 restoration. The level of comfort implied by the presence of the fireplace and garderobe shows that the Carisbrooke gatehouse housed someone important: the key location of medieval gatehouses, at the most vulnerable point of the defences, meant that they were prominent, high-status buildings, and often contained living accommodation for an important official.

The doorway at the front of the room leads to the drum towers. The medieval arrangements of this part of the gatehouse are unclear, as much of the masonry here dates to Percy Stone's restoration. The northern drum tower at this level has a good example of a medieval arrow slit. The southern drum tower has been used to house a spiral metal stair leading back down to the gate-passage. This was once the entrance to the Isle of Wight Museum, which opened in 1898 and was housed here until 1951.

Immediately inside the gatehouse to the south is the 16th-century guardhouse, from which the castle guards carried out their duties, and which is now used for exhibitions. The ruined building on the bank behind the guardhouse was an armoury of the same date. Further structures which were built into the ramparts on the north side of the gate-passage have disappeared.

2 CURTAIN WALL

By 1136, the stone curtain wall had been constructed on top of the massive earth banks and mound of the Norman castle. From the wall-walk along the top of the walls there are good views outwards which emphasize the central and dominating position of the castle within the Isle of Wight. It is also possible to get a good impression from here of the artillery fortress added around the medieval castle between 1597 and 1602.

Projecting towers, which provided additional protection, were probably added to the walls at the outset. None were built along the north side of the curtain wall because the hill is so steep and difficult to scale on that side, while the gatehouse would have allowed archers to cover much of the west curtain. There were towers at both angles of the south curtain wall as well as one in its centre. These were square, projecting slightly in front of the curtain wall and open to the inside of the castle (or filled in with timber). By the 16th

century, their outer faces were covered in white render. The back of the central tower was demolished in the 16th century, and the curtain wall was built across it.

Both the angle towers were reduced in height in 1587 and encased in 'knights', or artillery bastions. These were an early Elizabethan attempt to improve the defence of the castle against the threat of artillery at the time of the Spanish Armada. More work was carried out on them in 1601–2, following further Spanish threats. With their shallow pointed shape and short flanks, they were designed to carry guns providing both flanking fire along the curtain walls and outward fire at an attacking enemy (see page 21). The south-west bastion had five embrasures (openings) for guns, one on each face and one at its apex.

The east curtain would have been protected by the south-east angle tower and also by the keep on the motte. Originally the keep was totally separated from the rest of the castle by a massive ditch at least 4m deep. A further tower, which once stood on a small mound at the end of the original curtain wall opposite the motte to provide additional protection, disappeared long ago.

Facing page: The gate-passage, showing one of the portcullis slots. The small door leads via a passage into a guardroom on the ground floor of the drum tower

Below: An archer with a crossbow, from the early 14th-century Luttrell Psalter. The arrowloops along the wall-walk at Carisbrooke would have allowed archers to fire at attackers from relative safety

Left: The south curtain wall, which has projecting towers at both angles and at its centre

The motte ditch was partially infilled in the 14th century, possibly in 1335 when other improvements were made to the defences; a further stretch of curtain wall was built across it and up the side of the motte, completing the circuit of wall. At the same time, a small tower was added on the side of the former ditch.

The north curtain wall runs behind the great hall (page 11) and Carey's Mansion (page 15). In the medieval period and later there were many structures built into the rampart bank supporting the curtain wall. The first floor of Carey's Mansion ran along the terrace below the wall-walk, encasing the bailey bank in masonry. From this part of the wall-walk there are good views of Carisbrooke village and the mill pond. A Roman villa, which may have been one of the sources for Roman building material found in Norman earthworks in the castle, was found in the garden of one of the houses backing on to the brook.

▣ ▤ MOTTE AND KEEP

The keep was the ultimate refuge of the castle. Its other uses are uncertain, but the fragmentary remains of its buildings suggest that it may have been used at times for accommodation. It stands in the north-east corner of the castle, and is approached by climbing up the motte via 71 stairs.

Excavation has shown that the motte was built of alternating horizontal layers of loose and rammed chalk, with a foundation of stones, mainly flint. We do not know what structures crowned the motte when it was first built in about 1100, but there was probably some kind of timber tower. The motte was initially broader than it is today and its ditch wider. The original outer edge of the ditch has been found under the building which is now the tea room.

By 1136 the castle was described as having been 'strongly fortified in stone'. This work, which was carried out by Baldwin de Redvers, Richard de Redvers' heir, included the curtain walls of both the bailey and the motte. The present curtain wall of the keep must be part of that work, as it is similar both in style and in the stone used to the main curtain wall, except on its south side, which was possibly rebuilt in the 14th century.

Because the motte would not have carried the weight of a great stone tower, de Redvers built what is known as a shell keep. This was a

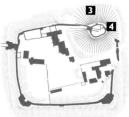

simple wall around the top of the motte, with lean-to buildings against its inner face. The keep walls may have been higher originally than they are now. The walls of even this relatively lightweight construction had to be buttressed in later centuries to prevent collapse.

In about 1335, when the castle's defences were upgraded in response to threats from the French, the keep too was improved defensively. Possibly at this time, the south side of the motte was scraped back and the motte ditch partially filled. This would

Left: The motte at Carisbrooke was built with alternating horizontal layers of loose and rammed chalk above a base layer of angular flints. This gave stability to the structure, and follows the practice shown here in the Bayeux Tapestry
Below: The keep and motte seen from the air

Facing page: The northern curtain wall and wall-walk, seen from the entrance to the keep gatehouse

Beneath the Inner Bailey

Excavations at Carisbrooke beneath the present inner bailey have found evidence of activity dating back to the sixth century, when the hilltop was the site of a small pagan cemetery (see page 25). Traces of a 10th-century Saxon settlement, the first post-Conquest castle and the later Norman castle have also been discovered from limited excavation. None of these early remains is now visible.

A The whole area of the inner bailey lies within the banks and wall of an 11th-century Saxon fort (see page 21). Traces of large timber buildings from this time have been found under the lawn.

B There is also evidence for the Norman castle created within this fort soon after 1066, in the form of two massive ditches curving across the lawn and under the main courtyard. These ditches created an inner bailey within the north-east corner of the Saxon fort.

C Buildings of the motte-and-bailey castle of about 1100 have also been found. The present great hall lies partly over a 12th-century building, and a structure of similar size was found to the south-west. Another formed the beginning of a range of buildings along the line of the east wall of the privy garden.

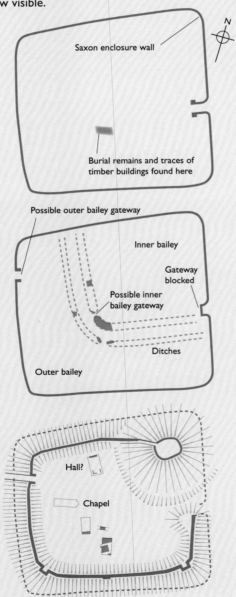

Saxon enclosure wall

Burial remains and traces of timber buildings found here

Possible outer bailey gateway

Inner bailey

Gateway blocked

Possible inner bailey gateway

Ditches

Outer bailey

Hall?

Chapel

Found in excavation

have provided space for the L-shaped range of buildings in the south-east corner of the castle. The keep gatehouse was certainly added at this time, giving further protection at the point of entry. It was vaulted in stone to minimize the risk of fire and would have had a fighting platform on its roof. Sited as it was on the edge of the motte, it had to be buttressed to prevent collapse.

Stairs against the curtain wall lead up to the gatehouse roof and to the keep wall-walk. There are magnificent views from here across the Solent as far as the mainland, as well as across the island. Almost opposite the gatehouse there is a garderobe shaft at wall-walk level, with another immediately below it; both are contained in a small projecting tower, and would have emptied onto the slope of the motte. Part of the stone seat in the upper garderobe survives. There is a third garderobe just north of the keep gatehouse.

The original internal arrangements of the keep are unclear. Two parallel walls now form a corridor running across it, but they date to the 16th century. The garderobe inserted into the east side of the curtain wall is earlier, as are the two back-to-back fireplaces to its left. One of these fireplaces also has an oven, so this room may have been a kitchen. The well in the room to the left of the passage appears to be original. This may be the well that ran dry in 1136, demonstrating the problems of water supply on this chalk hilltop. As a result, Baldwin de Redvers was forced to surrender the castle to King Stephen (see page 27). The well was dug to a depth of at least 48m (its current depth) to reach water. The various sockets in the wall next to it are evidence of a winch arrangement for raising water.

5 INNER BAILEY

Since at least the late 13th century the principal buildings of the castle have been arranged around an informal courtyard. This area is bounded to the east by the great hall, its attached chamber block (known as the Constable's Lodging) and the well house. The north side is dominated by the ruins of Carey's Mansion, which was built in 1584–6 but overlies earlier structures. To the west are the gatehouse and the 16th-century guardhouse. From at least the 14th century there was an L-shaped range of service buildings in the south-east corner of the bailey. This range, heavily modified, still survives. The south-west corner of the bailey was already separated from the rest of the castle and associated with the chapel of St Nicholas from the 12th century. While the basic plan of the inner bailey was established in the Middle Ages, the walls that now reinforce this layout were not all in place until the late 18th century.

6 GREAT HALL

The present great hall was built by Countess Isabella de Fortibus or one of her predecessors. Isabella was the last of the de Redvers family to hold the Isle of Wight, which she did from 1263 to 1293, and she was an exceptionally active builder.

As the hub of the castle's domestic life, the hall was never a completely free-standing building but was linked to its kitchen, which stood on the site of the later Carey's Mansion. At either end of the hall there were private domestic apartments for the lord of the castle and his or her close family and associates. Countess Isabella built her chapel onto the south-east corner of the hall and had further rooms to the east of that.

In the 13th century, the hall was a single-storey building, lower than it is now, over an undercroft. From the porch, the hall is entered by what used to be a screens passage, separating the service areas to the left from the body of the hall to the right. The hall would have looked very different then. It was open to the roof, and at the southern end there would have been a dais for the high

table where the lord would have eaten on great occasions; behind it, a doorway (now blocked) led to his private apartments. The main medieval feature surviving in the hall is the great fireplace inserted by William de Montacute, earl of Salisbury and lord of the island from 1386 to 1397, when the hall was already a century old. This was rediscovered by Philip Hardwick, an architect employed by the Office of Works in 1856 to carry out restoration work. Montacute's fireplace blocked one of the original 13th-century two-light lancet windows of the hall, which was revealed behind it during the restoration work.

The biggest changes to the hall were made in the 1580s by Sir George Carey, captain of the island from 1583 to 1603. He inserted an upper floor, raising the walls and the roof to make room for it. At the far end of the screens passage is a doorway giving access to a late 16th-century staircase to this upper floor, and to the rooms built in the north-east angle of the hall. The upper floor remains close to Carey's original design: it is partitioned into two rooms, both with fireplaces, and leading into small rooms on either side off the north end of the hall.

From 1647 to 1648 the hall range was used as a prison for Charles I, whose successive bedrooms were in the chamber blocks at either end. From

Facing page: The keep gatehouse, which was added in about 1335. Its outer doorway could be closed by a portcullis

Below: A lord and his guests feasting in a great hall, from a medieval French manuscript of about 1460

Right: William de Montacute's fine fireplace, added to the great hall in the late 14th century, blocked the lancet windows behind it. Previously the hall was probably heated by a fire in the centre of the room, from which smoke would have escaped through a hole in the roof

Far right: A cutaway reconstruction of the great hall and adjoining buildings as they may have looked in about 1400, after the alterations made by William de Montacute. To the right of the hall are St Peter's Chapel and the newly completed Constable's Lodging; to the left is the great chamber of Countess Isabella, which by this time was being used for storage

Below: The great hall and adjoining buildings today, seen from a similar angle to the reconstruction drawing opposite

1650 to 1653 it was used to imprison his daughter, Princess Elizabeth, who died here in 1650 at the age of 14, and his third son, Henry, duke of Gloucester, who went from here into exile.

The last significant changes were made by Lord Cutts, the governor of the castle from 1692 to 1706, who lowered the floor by 53cm to improve the height and appearance of the room. During the 18th century the earlier windows were replaced by up-to-date casements. The present windows were inserted in 1901 and the interior of the building was re-ordered for Princess Beatrice, who used Carisbrooke as a summer lodging from about 1913. The interior appearance of the building, including the panelling, is very much as it was in her time. Since 1951 the hall has housed the Carisbrooke Castle Museum.

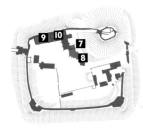

Right: The chapel of St Peter. Although partly obscured by the later staircase, enough survives of the 13th-century building to give some idea of its former grandeur

Below right: The Constable's Lodging, added to the south end of the great hall by William de Montacute in the late 14th century

Below: The late 13th-century squint, which allowed occupants of the castle to follow services in the chapel on the other side of the wall without having to leave their private accommodation. The squint was part of the arrangements that preceded the present late 14th-century Constable's Lodging, which had different floor levels

7 ST PETER'S CHAPEL

In 1270 Countess Isabella added the chapel of St Peter for her private use at the south-east end of the hall. It is entered directly from the hall and would have abutted a block of private lodgings to the south. The chapel was an elegant building, with arcades on the walls, lancet windows and a vaulted roof. In its south wall is a squint – a small, oblique opening in the wall – which would have allowed those within the chamber block to follow the service while remaining in the private apartment.

Carey removed the medieval vaulted roof and inserted a first floor within this space to provide extra rooms. In the late 17th century Lord Cutts in his turn inserted the present staircase to the upper floor, raising the roof in order to do so. He lined his stair hall with panelling which concealed what was left of the medieval structure. The medieval masonry was rediscovered in 1856 and since then the chapel has been displayed as it is now.

8 CONSTABLE'S LODGING

There would have been a building at the south-east corner of the great hall from at least 1270 when the chapel of St Peter was built, since the squint in the wall allowed views from here into

the chapel during services. The building may have provided private accommodation for Countess Isabella or one of her high officials, possibly the constable, who was responsible for the military administration of the castle. It was replaced in the 14th century in the time of William de Montacute, whose coat of arms appears on the buttress at the

Left: This drawing by John Livesay, dated 1798, shows the windows of the Constable's Lodging as they were when Charles I attempted to escape through the window of his first-floor bedroom while he was being held prisoner here (see pages 34–5). The window in its place now dates from the 19th century
Below: William de Montacute's coat of arms on the corner buttress of the Constable's Lodging
Bottom: Detail of the carving in one of the jambs of the 14th-century fireplace in the principal chamber of the Constable's Lodging, which served as Charles I's bedroom

south-west corner. The building has since been substantially altered and added to. It was originally entered from the great hall through a doorway within the thickness of the west wall of the chapel.

The Constable's Lodging was extended further to the south in the 15th century and then significantly modified in the 16th century by George Carey, who inserted a mezzanine floor into the principal first-floor chamber and panelled the remaining walls. Despite this, the original fireplace of the principal chamber survives, with geometric tracery in the angles of its jambs. The lower part of this room was Charles I's first bedroom, and his first escape attempt was from its window, since replaced by a later one.

The building now has three floors, with the principal apartment on the first floor, higher than the hall and linked to it via Lord Cutts's staircase. The Constable's Lodging as it now appears is principally the result of Hardwick's restoration of 1856. At that time, the Constable's Lodging formed the house for the keeper of the castle. Hardwick removed Carey's mezzanine floor to restore the dimensions of the first-floor rooms as built by Montacute. He also replaced the windows, which were in a variety of styles, with the present

ones, reusing some original surviving features, and removed some later additions to the building. The octagonal flat-roofed extension and porch were added in 1901 and the interiors were refitted when Carisbrooke became Princess Beatrice's summer home.

9 10 CAREY'S MANSION AND NORTH RANGE

Opposite St Nicholas's Chapel is Carey's Mansion, built between 1584 and 1586 by George Carey. He was cousin to Elizabeth I (1558–1603), and built the mansion to help provide accommodation sufficient for his rank and his household.

The mansion originally had an impressive façade to the courtyard, with two great bays rising to the eaves of the building (see page 16). It would thus have been on a par with many country houses built during Elizabeth's reign. It is still possible to see the two bays and the central door and passageway. In the end walls are the fireplaces of some of the 13 rooms recorded in the building. The mansion was built against and on top of the castle rampart, so that the northern part of its first floor was lit by large windows cut through the curtain wall. In Carey's day, this floor may have

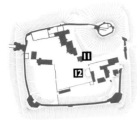

Right: A reconstruction of Carey's Mansion as it may have looked in about 1590; the photograph below shows the mansion and neighbouring buildings from a similar angle today. The mansion, built in the 1580s, was of two storeys and had 13 chambers

Carey's Mansion and the north range

A Entrance to Carey's Mansion

B Bay windows

C Possible long gallery

D 13th-century window seat (see page 28)

E Window of Charles I's second escape attempt (see page 34)

formed a long gallery, used for exercise and recreation. The foundations seen in the grass belong to earlier medieval buildings on this site. By 1723 a survey records that the mansion, then known as the Officers' Quarters, had fallen into ruin and had been demolished, presumably because such extensive accommodation was no longer needed.

East of Carey's Mansion at first-floor level are the ruins of the buildings that abutted the north end of the hall. In the 1270s Countess Isabella built her great chamber, or principal private apartment, here: this was a time when the rich were seeking greater privacy and creating chambers for their personal use. The windows with stepped seating would have given her views across the north of the island to the mainland. Thirteenth-century building accounts suggest that the windows here were glazed, an unusual luxury at the time. This area of the castle has been much altered, being used for storage in the 14th century and becoming in Carey's time a kitchen and service rooms with bedrooms above. Some of the fireplaces and the oven date from this use. Charles I made a second bid to escape the castle from one of the windows on an upper floor in this area, after he was moved here following his first bungled escape attempt.

11 12 WELL HOUSE AND DONKEY CENTRE

The well in the inner bailey courtyard was dug after the one in the keep failed in 1136, which led to the surrender of the castle. The courtyard well is 49m deep: its upper part is lined with masonry, while the lower part is cut through solid chalk. It still holds water to a depth of about 12m). By 1292, when repairs were made, there was a well house over the well, with a treadwheel to raise buckets of water. According to the building accounts, the present well house and treadwheel were built by Sir George Carey in 1587. At about the same time he built a large underground water cistern west of the Constable's Lodging. This has been discovered by excavation, although nothing is now visible. The well house and treadwheel have remained in use ever since, although since the castle was connected to the water mains in the early 20th century the wheel has only been used for demonstration to visitors.

Originally the wheel was probably turned by prisoners. The first record of any other motive power comes from the observations of the inveterate traveller Celia Fiennes in 1696 that water was drawn by a 'horse or ass'. From then on donkeys seem to have been used, although until 1880 only one was kept at the castle. Now the work is shared by a team of donkeys. Their training takes about seven months and they work for only two hours each day to demonstrate the use of the wheel. The Donkey Centre has a small exhibition about the donkeys of Carisbrooke.

Above: The well house and its donkeys have long been a visitor attraction at Carisbrooke, as is shown by this late 19th-century engraving
Below left: *A donkey working the treadwheel*

🔢 SOUTH-EAST RANGE

The south-east part of the castle is dominated by two buildings forming an L-shape. Built originally in the 14th century, they revet a small mound which originally ended the bailey bank on the motte ditch, thus creating between them a small yard at first-floor level. In the north wall of the northern building can be seen the relieving arches built to carry the weight of the stone building down through the fill of the motte ditch to bedrock.

These structures were extensively rebuilt in 1856. During their history they have been service buildings and barracks, and they now house the castle tea room and education centre. In front of them is a small walled yard. The wooden buildings against the walls were built as service buildings and house the castle fire station, which was created before the First World War and still contains the firefighting equipment for the castle, since the castle gateway is too narrow for a fire engine. These buildings also now contain an exhibition on the Carisbrooke donkeys, while the most recent addition is a new donkey stable.

🔢 CHAPEL OF ST NICHOLAS

There has been a long sequence of chapels dedicated to St Nicholas roughly where the present chapel now stands. The chapel was always a parish church in its own right, and even in the medieval period was administered separately from the rest of the castle.

A chapel was first mentioned in Domesday Book in 1086, although no traces of that building survive. It was replaced by an early medieval chapel, the foundations of which can be seen at the base of the walls of the present chapel. This medieval chapel was rebuilt in 1738 and dismantled in 1856.

The present building dates to 1904, and was designed by Percy Stone to commemorate the 250th anniversary of Charles I's execution in 1649. The ante-chapel contains a contemporary bust of him attributed to Bernini (see page 3).

Entered through a porch at the north-west corner, the chapel has a richly decorated interior which is a great contrast to the rather plain, medieval-style exterior. This interior was not intended in the original design but results from the decision after the First World War to make the chapel into the Isle of Wight's war memorial.

Left: The organ in St Nicholas's Chapel, which was donated by Edward VII (1901–10) from the Rolls Chapel in Chancery Lane, London. The ceiling was painted in 1925

Below: A late 19th-century photograph showing the chapel after it was dismantled in 1856 and before its rebuilding in 1904

Facing page: The chapel interior looking east. The chapel serves as the island's war memorial and the woodwork is from HMS Nettle, which was one of the last of the wooden warships, launched in 1831

The names of the 2,000 island men killed in both world wars are inscribed on stone panels between the windows, while the altar painting was commissioned by Princess Beatrice in memory of her youngest son, Maurice, who was killed at Ypres in 1914. The statues on either side of the altar are of the patron saints of island churches.

Right: The Princess Beatrice Garden, designed in 2009 and inspired by the garden created for Princess Beatrice from 1913

Below right: A lady in a garden, from a manuscript of about 1470. In the late 13th century Isabella de Fortibus created a garden at Carisbrooke, which is known to have contained a sundial, a herb garden and a fish tank; its site is unknown

⓫ PRIVY GARDEN

Behind the chapel to the south is the privy garden. From the 12th century, this area was partly cut off from the rest of the castle by a range of buildings along the line of the garden wall, and by the chapel itself. The area might once have been a cemetery for the chapel, but from the 17th century it was a garden for captains and governors of Carisbrooke. Depending on their horticultural inclinations, it served both for pleasure and as a kitchen garden.

From 1913 it became Princess Beatrice's private or privy garden, and this has been the inspiration for the new Princess Beatrice Garden, designed in 2009 by the garden designer Chris Beardshaw as the result of a bequest. The design is based on the original layout and uses plants that reflect the spirit of the period. Divided into four quarters, the garden has a fountain as its centrepiece; there are formal clipped hedges and fruit trees contained in large planters. Architectural details from the adjoining chapel of St Nicholas and elements of the princess's blue, red and gold heraldic crest are woven into the design.

OUTER DEFENCES

16 Saxon Lower Enclosure

The earliest defence of the hilltop was a near-rectangular enclosure dating to about 1000, now known as the lower enclosure. This was a chalk bank which was subsequently faced with a wall believed to be around 3m thick. There was one known entrance into the Saxon enclosure on the east side.

The banks of this late Saxon fort were largely buried under the bank of the Norman motte-and-bailey castle. It is possible, however, to see parts of the facing wall of the Saxon lower enclosure at points around the base of the Norman bank. The best stretches can be seen by looking back from the bowling green. The wall of the lower enclosure here is built on base courses of very large stones with smaller masonry above. At the north end of this stretch of wall (at the base of the Norman motte), there is a small bastion-like projection. In the centre the wall curves from both directions under the later Norman banks. This is believed to be the beginnings of a long gate-passage into the Saxon enclosure. The inner end of this entrance was found during excavations 16m to the west, far below the present tea room.

Part of the lower enclosure wall

A Rectangular blocks at base of wall
B Semicircular bastion
C Curved wall at entrance to lower enclosure
D 14th-century curtain wall built over the lower enclosure and ditch

17 18 Artillery Fortifications and Bowling Green

Carisbrooke remained of military importance for much longer than most English castles. Because of its location it was important for coastal defence, particularly during the Spanish wars in the reign of Elizabeth I. As a result, it underwent significant refortification in 1587 and between 1597 and 1602.

High medieval defensive walls were vulnerable to gunfire, and the new defences were low in profile to withstand artillery fire and had thick banks to absorb cannon balls. They were also designed to carry artillery, to fire both outwards at enemy siege works and along the defences to

Left: The Elizabethan additions to the castle, shown here, transformed it into an up-to-date artillery fortress. Five large arrowhead bastions were equipped to cover the whole perimeter of the castle with their range of fire. Their outward-facing sides carried batteries of guns to shoot at enemy positions, while flanker batteries on their short sides could sweep the defences themselves with fire

■ 1587 defences
■ 1597–1602 defences

North bastion

North-west bastion

West bastion

Bowling green

Flanker batteries

South-west bastion

East bastion

0   100 metres

0   100 yards

prevent attackers from storming them. This led to the development of bastioned defences, normally with arrow-shaped bastions.

As well as the two 'knights' added to the curtain wall (see page 7), the refortifications in 1587 involved additional earthworks outside the castle on the south, east and possibly north sides, to provide protection against gunfire. Of these, probably the only survivor is a substantial earthwork east of the castle, with small bastions at its north-east and south-east corners. It was later reshaped to form a bowling green for the entertainment of Charles I during his imprisonment at Carisbrooke, probably by the creation of terraces on the inner faces of the banks. The cannon on the two bastions are 19th-century naval guns given to the castle in the early 20th century.

The other outworks of 1587 must have been swept away when a full-scale artillery fortress was built around the castle between 1597 and 1602. Designed by an Italian engineer, Federigo Gianibelli, this fortress was roughly rectangular, with bastions at each corner and a fifth in the middle of the west front to protect the entrance to the castle. The ramparts are massive chalk banks, almost one mile in circumference, faced by stone walls and fronted by a deep ditch.

The east and south fronts were clearly seen as the most vulnerable, since the bastions here were equipped with two-storey flanker batteries to maximize fire along these faces of the ramparts. In all, there were four such flanker batteries. The details can be best seen in the east flanker of the

south-west bastion. The battery was built in chalk with greensand facing blocks. The upper part of the present wall across the battery is a later decorative feature: the original front wall only came up to the chamfered plinth and was 2.2m wide, with embrasures for two cannon. In the centre of the rear part of the battery a masonry pier supported a vaulted upper floor for two more cannon. The spaces underneath would have provided storage and shelter for troops.

The batteries do not seem to have had a long life and were probably demolished some time after the mid-17th century. This was not the last use of the castle for artillery, however: in the 19th century Carisbrooke was the base for batteries of the Isle of Wight Artillery Militia, a predecessor of today's Territorial Army. Their barracks were in the L-shaped range in the inner bailey and guns were mounted on the north-west bastion for training. Traces of their mountings survive.

Left: While Charles I was a prisoner he developed a passion for bowls, and the bowling green at Carisbrooke was created especially for his entertainment within a 16th-century earthwork
Below: A reconstruction of the east flanker battery on the south-west bastion, which held guns on two levels to fire along the face of the rampart. On the south side of the battery was a sloping passage leading to a sally port or side entrance which gave access to the ditches
Below left: The battery seen from a similar angle today

Facing page: The ramparts on the north side of the castle, seen from the wall-walk. The long, low banks and ditches were faced with stone walls to provide maximum protection against gunfire

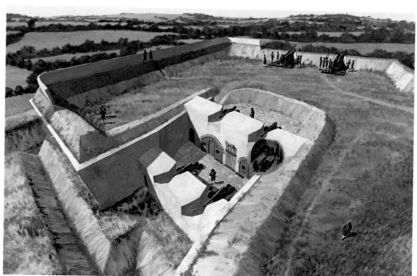

History

There has been a fortress at Carisbrooke since before the Norman Conquest, but the present castle with its massive earthworks and keep was begun about 1100, when the Isle of Wight was granted to the de Redvers family. In the late 13th century the last of the de Redvers, Countess Isabella de Fortibus, transformed the castle into a magnificent residence.

Carisbrooke experienced its only siege in 1377, rebuffing a French raiding force. Under Elizabeth I, faced with the threat of further Spanish attacks after the Armada had passed unnervingly close in 1588, Carisbrooke was one of the few castles to be wholly refortified with vast artillery defences. During the Civil War Carisbrooke housed its most prestigious, if unwilling, resident, Charles I, who was imprisoned here in 1647–8 shortly before his execution.

Thereafter Carisbrooke faded from the national stage, but it retained a ceremonial role well into the 20th century as a residence of the governors of the Isle of Wight, including Princess Beatrice, Queen Victoria's youngest daughter.

EARLY HISTORY

The area around Carisbrooke has been an important focus of settlement since the Roman period, when there were at least three villas in the vicinity of Carisbrooke and Newport, one of which lay in the valley below the castle. This suggests considerable wealth in the area, although there is no secure evidence of Roman occupation on the castle hilltop itself.

The earliest direct evidence of human activity on the Carisbrooke hill is a small sixth-century pagan Saxon cemetery, which was revealed during excavations beneath the inner bailey lawn. The cemetery presumably belonged to a settlement in one of the valleys below the hill. Three graves had survived later disturbance. One of them was that of a young man, who had been buried with an imitation Byzantine coin in his mouth, together with a glass drinking bowl, a drinking horn, a large bronze bowl, a set of ivory playing counters and a bucket. This was an exceptional burial, both in the richness of the grave goods found with the body and in the absence of weapons, but the reasons for this are unclear.

A century or so later, there was a major Saxon settlement in the valley to the west of Carisbrooke; the coins found in the area show that it had wide connections, rivalling those of the

trading centre at Hamwih (Southampton) on the mainland. The next known activity on the hilltop, however, dates to about 1000, a time of Viking raids around the coast of southern England. Between 998 and 1009 Vikings based themselves on the Isle of Wight four times to raid the mainland, and other Viking raids took place later in the 11th century.

The response to these raids was the fortification of the kingdom of Wessex with many fortresses (or burhs) as centres of resistance and refuge for the local population. It is likely that Carisbrooke was built as the burh for the Isle of

Left: Vikings attacking a Saxon burh, from a manuscript of about 1130 illuminated at Bury St Edmunds, Suffolk
Below: Remains of the Saxon lower enclosure wall of about 1000 are visible on the west side of the castle near the base of the Norman castle bank

Facing page: Charles I at his trial in January 1649, after Edward Bower (d. 1667). Bower probably worked up his portrait from drawings made at Westminster Hall during the trial

Above: *The motte, built in about 1100, probably by Richard de Redvers, lord of the Isle of Wight; the stone walls of the keep were built by his son, Baldwin, by 1136. The Saxon lower enclosure wall can be seen at the base of the motte*

Wight and that this was the first occupation of the hilltop. It was fortified with a roughly rectangular chalk bank with rounded corners, later faced with a stone wall; this so-called lower enclosure can be seen in places at the base of the Norman castle banks. The fortification enclosed large timber buildings and was entered via a gateway on the eastern side (see page 10).

THE CASTLE OF THE CONQUEST

Following their victory at the battle of Hastings in 1066, the Normans urgently needed to secure themselves against revolt and against other potential invaders. Along the south coast, King William I (1066–87) created a series of large and powerful baronies for his most loyal followers to prevent invasion by others. They built castles which acted as centres of power and residence as well as garrisoned fortifications. The Isle of Wight was granted to William FitzOsbern, cousin and close supporter of the king and one of the great magnates of early Norman England. He probably built a castle at Carisbrooke soon after the Conquest to defend against any overseas attack.

A castle at Carisbrooke with a church inside it is first recorded in the Domesday survey of 1086. This was not the castle we now see, but an adaptation of the existing Saxon defences. Reuse of earlier fortifications was a common Norman response to the urgent need for strongholds, as can be seen at nearby Portchester Castle, which the Normans built within one corner of the Roman fort.

Inside the existing Saxon fort, two ditches were dug, perhaps successively, to cut off the north-west quadrant of the burh and form the inner bailey or courtyard of the new castle (see page 10). The outer ditch was about 2m deep while the inner one was 4–5m deep and 6m wide. The remainder of the enclosure would have consisted of an outer bailey with a gateway probably on the site of the present gatehouse. The earlier burh gateway on the east side would have been buried by the inner bailey rampart. An early phase of the chapel of St Nicholas may have stood on part of the site of the present chapel. Nothing of this castle, which would have been built of wood and earth, can be seen above ground.

THE DE REDVERS' CASTLE

William FitzOsbern's heir rebelled against William I and was deprived of his lands, so from 1075 to 1100 the castle at Carisbrooke was held directly by the Crown. In 1100 Henry I became king after the death of his brother, William Rufus, in spite of the claims to the throne of his eldest brother, Robert. At the beginning of his reign Henry needed to bolster and reward his supporters to strengthen his power base, particularly along the south coast, to prevent invasion from Normandy, which was ruled by Robert until 1106, when Henry conquered it. Henry granted the Isle of Wight and extensive estates in Devon to Richard de Redvers, one of his followers and supporters before he came to the throne, and it was held by the de Redvers family until 1293. It was almost certainly Richard who built the motte-and-bailey castle, with its entrance on the site of the present gatehouse, which has shaped all later development on the hilltop. In his time, the defences would have been of timber. Richard died in 1107 and was succeeded by his son Baldwin, who must have built the stone walls of the bailey and keep, since by 1136 the castle is recorded as a strongly fortified stone building.

Little is known of the interior of the castle at this time. The chapel of St Nicholas was presumably on its present site, though the earliest visible remains are at least 100 years later. South of the chapel, a stone building partially cut off the south-west corner of the castle, later the privy garden. There was another stone building in the middle of the inner bailey and probably another whose undercroft survives below the present great hall.

After Henry I's death in 1135, Baldwin de Redvers supported the king's daughter, Matilda, in her claim to the throne when the king's nephew Stephen took it for himself, resulting in civil war. In 1136 Baldwin probably intended to defend Carisbrooke, but the failure of the castle well (presumably that in the keep, which was then the only one in the castle) meant that he was forced to surrender to King Stephen at Southampton. He did not recover his lands until 1153, after which they remained in the hands of his descendants until the death of the last of them, Countess Isabella de Fortibus (see page 28), who sold them to Edward I on her deathbed in 1293.

Little is known of the development of the castle before Isabella inherited it in 1263. An inventory taken in 1294 tells us that the castle had four chambers at an upper level next to a hall over an undercroft, a great chapel (the chapel of St Nicholas) belonging to Quarr Abbey, a small chapel, a great kitchen, a chamber for the constable over an undercroft and many other buildings. This is recognizably the outline of the castle that survives today and was largely Isabella's creation.

Left: A nobleman kneels to receive the sword of knighthood from a king
Below left: Matilda (1102–67), daughter of Henry I, depicted in an English manuscript of 1380. Baldwin de Redvers took Matilda's side in her unsuccessful claim to the throne against that of King Stephen, who was Henry I's nephew
Below: The arms of the de Redvers family, lords of Carisbrooke from 1100 until 1293

Above: A carved stone head at Christchurch Priory, Dorset, believed to be a portrait of Isabella de Fortibus
Right: This window with seating in the north wall was one of three similar windows in Isabella's great chamber, with views over the valley. The window was glazed, a great luxury at the time
Below right: A lady and her maid, from the 14th-century Luttrell Psalter

By her 26th birthday Isabella had become one of the great landowners in England of her day

Countess Isabella's Castle

Isabella inherited the estates of her husband, William de Fortibus, which lay mainly in the north of England, in 1260 at the age of 23. Two years later her brother, Baldwin de Redvers, died, possibly from poisoning, and she inherited his lands in the Isle of Wight, Hampshire and Devon. This meant that by her 26th birthday she had become one of the great landowners in England of her day, and she was to hold her estates until her death in 1293. It was unusual at that time for a woman to hold such great power, and in order to maintain and enforce her rights Isabella became fiercely litigious.

Many of her records survive, giving an exceptionally clear picture of the work she did at Carisbrooke. She made the castle her main residence and the administrative headquarters of her southern estates. During her tenure it must often have felt like a perpetual construction site, as buildings were constantly being altered, extended or erected from scratch to transform it into a residence befitting her status. She began by reordering the principal apartments of the castle. At one end of the hall she added the chapel of St Peter. At the other, northern end, she added a great chamber for herself, with windows looking out across the island. Later she built new apartments for the constable, an important official who carried out much of the administration of her estates, at the southern end of the hall, as well as a new kitchen for the hall in the area where Carey's Mansion later stood.

As well as detailing the new buildings, repairs and alterations, the accounts reveal some of the more ephemeral aspects of Isabella's castle: it had a sundial in a herb garden between the hall and the gatehouse, a fish tank or pool for keeping fish for food, and a prison.

THE LATE MEDIEVAL CASTLE

During the 14th century, the Hundred Years War with France (1337–1453) meant that the Isle of Wight was on the front line – possession of the island could give control of the Solent and access to central southern England. The French raided the island or the Solent five times between 1336 and 1370. In 1377 they landed in strength on the north coast of the island, destroyed the towns of Yarmouth and Francheville there, advanced on Carisbrooke and besieged it. In a colourful account of the siege written two centuries later, Sir John Oglander described how the French commander was killed by the bowman Peter de Heynoe, who had been observing the commander's movements, with a single shot, so bringing the siege to an end: 'and by that means brought the French to a composition to take 1000 marks to be gone'.

The French threat, combined with the fact that the lordship of the island was by that time effectively an appointment by the Crown, meant that the focus of work on the castle was mainly on its defences rather than its residential buildings. In 1335–6 the drum towers were added to the main gatehouse, which was probably originally built by Isabella. A small gatehouse was added to the keep. The drum towers were heightened again in about 1380 with a new upper stage including purpose-built gun loops, shaped like inverted keyholes. Domestic arrangements were not entirely neglected, however: William de Montacute, earl of Salisbury, who held the lordship of the island from 1386 to 1397, rebuilt the accommodation block (the Constable's Lodging) south of the great hall and remodelled the latter with a new fireplace and, presumably, new windows, since the fireplace blocked at least one of the existing windows (see page 12).

French raids on the island continued into the early 15th century, but for much of it lords of the island held office for short periods and generally lived elsewhere, visiting infrequently. There are few surviving accounts for the castle during this time.

'One Peter de Heynoe came to Sir Hugh Tyrell, then Captain of the Island, and told him he would undertake with his tiller bow to kill the commander of the French ... which on leave he killed out of a loophole on the west side of the castle' From Sir John Oglander's description of the French siege of 1377. This arrowloop on the west side of the castle has long been identified as Heynoe's loop in honour of the bowman

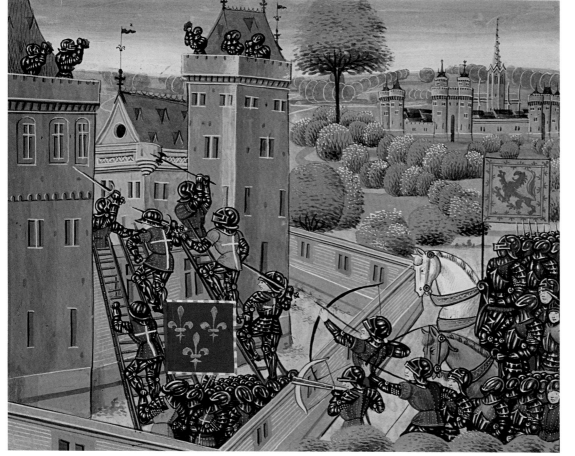

Left: The capture of Wark Castle, Northumberland, by the French and Scots, depicted in a manuscript of about 1460–80. The French besieged Carisbrooke in 1377 and continued to raid the Isle of Wight in the 15th century

netley   S Andros

Tychefylde

Rowner gosport

Stoke

Calfhards

hasellorde

stoke bay

falley

Bewley

the brables

west cow   est cow Meadehole

Showflyt Wotto hauen
quar

Whyppyngham ll   sande hed

park

gurney   flackfeyd   north wood   Ryde
nettelftone

parkehurft   Affie
worsley   miavett   S Elly

fhoflyt   newton

Newport

colburne   Casebroke

Areton.

thurley   Evtt
ma the kyngs pke   newchurch   Bradynge

fwenfton.

VECTA   Gascu.   Wyght.

Godshytt   Bmbryge   benbr

broke

Shorewell   ye

Rowner.   brykfton   Dynfley   kyngfton.

Motfiert   chet   Woluton   S
ronne   Whrtwell   Sanden bay.
Dynley

Apledor Coumbe
worsley

Chynkly   Chynkhuyg chyne.

Freshewar   Compto bay.
bay.   chale

Chale bay   S kataryne S laurens S Boniface
S hytt

Dounose.

In 1450 the inhabitants of the island petitioned Henry VI (1422–61) to take action since the castle was in a state of disrepair, and lacked a garrison and military supplies. From 1467 to 1483 its lord was Anthony Woodville, brother-in-law of Edward IV (1461–70 and 1471–83). He clearly spent money on the castle, since the machicolations on the gatehouse carry, now very faintly, his coat of arms. It was probably Woodville who extended the Constable's Lodging to the south.

CARISBROOKE UNDER THE TUDORS

In the first half of the 16th century the castle seems to have been somewhat neglected, despite renewed French threats. The captains of the island during this time mostly lived elsewhere. A changing defensive strategy under Henry VIII (1509–47) also affected the castle, as he invested in a major programme of coastal defences against the possibility of French invasion. On the Isle of Wight he built coastal forts at Yarmouth, East and West Cowes, St Helens and Sandown, with smaller blockhouses elsewhere. Carisbrooke Castle effectively became a munitions store. In 1545 the French landed on the island and apparently considered seizing it permanently, but in fact carried out only a short raid.

In 1583 Sir George Carey, later Lord Hunsdon, was appointed captain of the castle. As a cousin of Elizabeth I (1558–1603), he had a high opinion of his own importance. As well as regarding a

major castle such as Carisbrooke as a fitting residence for a great magnate, he also saw it as the focus of the island's defence against the Spanish, who contemplated seizing it in 1588 as part of the invasion which was the objective of the Spanish Armada. The island was again the planned target of the lesser known Spanish expeditions of 1596 and 1597, although these were both dispersed by storms before they reached the English Channel.

A survey of 1583 had found that the castle had virtually no fit accommodation and that its store of armaments was largely unserviceable. It was said that 'we finde verie smale store of lodginge for his

Above: The launching of English fireships on the Spanish Armada, depicted in a Flemish painting of about 1605. The Spanish Armada was sighted from the Isle of Wight on the morning of 26 July 1588. Sir George Carey, captain of the castle under Elizabeth I, later described how 'this morning began a great fight between both fleets … [which] were out of sight by three in the afternoon'
Left: The seal of Sir George Carey

Facing page: The Vecta Wight map of 1593, showing Carisbrooke Castle at the centre of the island

'He was a most free man in his house-keeping, and his meat was always served up to his table with a consort of wind and still music'

Sir George Carey

Above right: Detail from a portrait of about 1596 of Sir Henry Unton showing a lord holding a banquet, while a masque is performed accompanied by musicians. Sir George Carey often hosted lavish banquets at Carisbrooke
Above: A 16th-century miniature portrait of Sir George Carey

Sir George Carey was a cousin of Elizabeth I (as a grandson of Mary, sister of Anne Boleyn). He was appointed captain of the Isle of Wight in 1583 at the age of 34 and held the post until his death in 1603. Closely linked to the Queen's Council, he entertained many of its members, including the earl of Leicester, at Carisbrooke.

Carey dominated the island for 20 years as its captain and as vice-admiral, which meant that he controlled the local admiralty court. Admiralty courts had jurisdiction over shipping and dealt with complaints of piracy and other breaches of maritime law. At this time the Isle of Wight had a reputation as a centre of piracy and privateering: Carey was among those who commissioned privateering expeditions – government-licensed but privately funded raids against Spanish shipping – and with his associates invested in expeditions that went as far as the Caribbean. He was also a patron of the arts and artists, including the poet Thomas Nashe and composers such as John Dowland.

When the island was threatened by invasion Carey took the lead in organizing its defences. As well as fortifying Carisbrooke, he carried out work on some of the coastal defences and refurbished the beacon chains that formed part of an early warning system against invading fleets right around the English coast. He organized and trained the militia to defend the island and virtually nominated three of the island's six MPs to Parliament.

Not one to brook opposition, Carey once described himself as 'your frynde if fryndlie used' after he had jailed one of the local gentry who had objected to his arbitrary behaviour. He was reputed, though, to be a generous host, frequently entertaining all the island gentry to lavish banquets:

'His weekly expense in wheat-corn and pastry was constantly three quarters, but when lords and ladies were there ... he spent treble as much, for then he would have all the gentlemen of the Island their wives also there. He was a most free man in his house-keeping, and his meat was always served up to his table with a consort of wind and still music.'

He did not forget the servants: 'The laundry was never without a hogshead of wine and a cold pasty of venison for the maids.' But according to Sir John Oglander, who wrote this account, which was probably derived from stories told him by his father, Carey's relationship with his wife, Elizabeth (who was a literary patron in her own right), was not always harmonious:

'His wife was daughter to my Lord Spencer, a very handsome lady, and so was he a very personable fine gentleman, and would to God they could have had that opinion one of the other.'

familye and howsholde … by reason that no Captain hast dwelt there these xxxti yeres'. Carey remedied this with extensive building works. The hall was heightened and divided into two floors, as were the adjoining St Peter's Chapel and the great chamber in the Constable's Lodging. Abutting the northern inner bailey wall he added a new building, which was, in effect, a mansion in its own right with 13 rooms, perhaps including a long gallery (see page 16). He also rebuilt the 13th-century well house and installed the present treadmill to raise water.

Defence of the castle was not neglected. In response to the invasion scare of 1587 which culminated in the arrival of the Spanish Armada the following year, Carey added small bastions (knights) around two angle towers of the inner bailey wall and probably created a large outwork (barbican) to the east of the inner bailey (later converted into the bowling green). There may also have been other earthworks, now lost, intended to make the castle more fit to withstand a Spanish artillery attack.

In the next Spanish invasion scare of 1596–7, Carey galvanized the Queen's Council into sanctioning the transformation of Carisbrooke

Castle into an artillery fort and the island gentry into contributing to its costs. The new defences were designed by an Italian engineer and expert on fortification, Federigo Gianibelli. Work began in 1597 and the new fortifications were finally completed in 1602, although they were never used in conflict. They were a massive undertaking with a circumference of nearly a mile, and defended by five bastions. On the more vulnerable southern and eastern sides, the bastions had double-decker flanker batteries to maximize gunfire against any enemy who assaulted the ramparts.

Left: The Carisbrooke parish gun, made in 1549, and now in the Carisbrooke Castle Museum. Each parish on the Isle of Wight had such a gun for defence

Below left: Detail from an engraving of a lost wall-painting of about 1545–8 depicting the battle of the Solent in 1545. Troops like those shown here defending Portsmouth harbour may have served at Carisbrooke

Below: An engraving from an Italian manual of 1564, entitled 'How to adjust the firing posts and how to choose the angle of the walls'. The artillery defences at Carisbrooke were designed by the Italian engineer Federigo Gianibelli; such defences, based on mathematical principles, originated in Italy

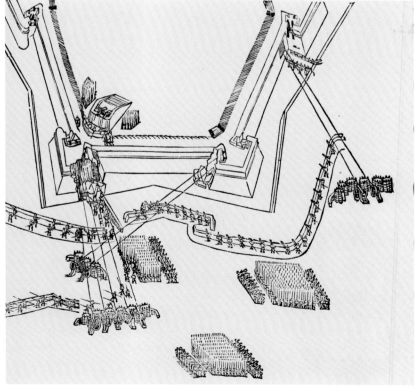

On the night of
20 March 1648
Charles attempted
to climb out
through the
window of his
bedchamber, but
became wedged
between the bars

A Royal Prisoner at Carisbrooke

Charles I was a prisoner at Carisbrooke from
22 November 1647 until 6 September 1648.
Nonetheless, he was housed in some state and
had the use of the Constable's Lodging and the
upper floor of the hall. For the first part of his
imprisonment he was allowed considerable
freedom, and many of his own household came to
the island to join him. The eastern outwork was
converted into a bowling green for his use (see
page 23). His first bedchamber was in what is
now the lower part of the great chamber in the
Constable's Lodging.

During his time at Carisbrooke, Charles
negotiated both with Parliament and with the Scots
to achieve a settlement which would return some
power to him and allow him to maintain his throne.
Once it became clear that no progress towards
this would be made in the negotiations, he was
imprisoned more strictly and his own attendants
were removed. Despite this, he was still able to
contact supporters outside the castle, first through
his own attendants, and, after they were sent away,
through secret messages carried by servants. It was
arranged that horses and a boat would be ready if
he could escape from the castle.

On the night of 20 March 1648 Charles
attempted to climb out through the window of his
bedchamber, but became wedged between the bars.
After this failed escape he was moved to another,
more secure bedchamber (now demolished) next
to the north curtain wall. A second attempt on
28 May 1648 was aborted after it was betrayed,
and extra sentries were posted below his window.

Charles was finally moved from the castle into
Newport on 6 September that year for negotiations
with Parliament; these were held in the old
grammar school, which still survives. After their
failure, he was moved by various stages to London,
where he was put on trial. He was eventually
executed in Whitehall on 30 January 1649.

THE CIVIL WAR AND AFTER

After peace was made with Spain in 1604, the immediate motivation for the work to improve the castle defences disappeared. Archaeological evidence suggests that the elaborate flanker batteries were demolished within 25 years of their construction. By 1623, when a survey was made, the castle was primarily the arsenal for all the island fortifications.

In September 1642 the simmering conflict between King Charles I and Parliament culminated in civil war. At the outset, Carisbrooke, with the rest of the island, was secured for Parliament when it was surrendered without bloodshed by the countess of Portland, wife of the absent governor of the Isle of Wight, and her garrison of 20 men to a much larger force led by the mayor of Newport. Philip Herbert, fourth earl of Pembroke, was appointed as the new governor for Parliament, and from then on Carisbrooke's principal function for the rest of the war was as a political prison for a few high status individuals.

The most famous prisoner held at Carisbrooke was the deposed Charles I. In November 1647 he managed to escape from Hampton Court Palace, where he had been held, effectively under house arrest, by Parliament since the previous year while it tried to decide his fate. He travelled to Titchfield House in Hampshire, and once there he opened negotiations with Colonel Robert Hammond, the Parliamentarian governor of the Isle of Wight but also brother to his chaplain, and thought to be a crypto-Royalist. Charles clearly believed that on the island he would have more freedom to negotiate with both Parliament and the Scots, as well as having a greater chance of fleeing to France if necessary. He arrived at Carisbrooke on 22 November and put himself under the protection of Hammond; but the latter, instead of helping him to get away, instead became his gaoler. Charles remained a prisoner here for nearly 10 months (see feature opposite).

The castle continued to be used as a prison for several years. Two of Charles's children, Princess Elizabeth and his third son, Prince Henry, were brought here in August 1650, after their father's execution in 1649, presumably because Carisbrooke was already fitted out to be a prison for notables. The 14-year-old Elizabeth died within weeks of her arrival, from a chill contracted while

playing bowls. Henry, duke of Gloucester, who was 10 years old when he arrived at the castle, remained a prisoner until February 1653 when he was allowed to join his family in exile in France. Other Royalists were imprisoned here during Oliver Cromwell's Protectorate (1650–60), but in 1660, with the restoration of Charles II to the throne, it was the turn of supporters of Parliament and the Protectorate to be held here.

Left: Colonel Robert Hammond, Charles I's rather reluctant gaoler at Carisbrooke, drawn by G P Harding (after C Johnson). While Charles was planning his second bid to escape from Carisbrooke, Hammond reputedly had wind of the plan: he visited Charles shortly before the planned time for the escape, and remarked courteously: 'I am come to take leave of your majesty, for I hear you are going away.' Hammond died in 1654 and is buried in St Thomas's Church, Newport

Below: A Victorian illustration of 14-year-old Princess Elizabeth, daughter of Charles I, on her deathbed at Carisbrooke in 1650

Right: Volunteer troops being awarded the Island Banner in 1798

'As brave and brainless as the sword he wears … and the vainest old fool alive'
Dean Swift describing Lord Cutts (above, in a portrait of about 1690), governor of Carisbrooke from 1692 to 1706. Cutts, one of Marlborough's generals, was believed by many to be a rash military commander

THE 18TH CENTURY: CARISBROOKE'S CHANGING ROLE

The significance of Carisbrooke Castle declined from the later 17th century. The Isle of Wight was a French target in times of war – an elaborate plan to seize it by *coup de main* was developed as late as 1778, during the American War of Independence, by Charles François Dumouriez, a French soldier of fortune and politician. But by that time there were other means of defending the island, in the form of modernized coastal forts and the existence of a strong Royal Navy. Carisbrooke retained a role as a stores depot for some time and later was a military hospital. Plans to add barracks to the castle in the 18th century came to nothing.

From time to time Carisbrooke was also still used as a residence by the governor of the Isle of Wight. This resulted in periodic investment in the buildings, but otherwise the castle seems to have decayed gently. During the tenure of Lord Cutts (1692–1706), who had been one of William III's companions in the Revolution of 1688 and was later one of the duke of Marlborough's generals, over £700 was spent on adapting the hall block. The floor of the hall was lowered to provide more headroom and a grand staircase

was inserted into the former chapel of St Peter, which was panelled throughout. Cutts also removed the mezzanine floor inserted by Carey into the great chamber of the Constable's Lodging. In 1724 a further £800 was spent on repairs to the castle during the governorship of Lord Cadogan (1715–26), perhaps the most important of Marlborough's generals. In 1738 Viscount Lymington demolished the chapel of St Nicholas and rebuilt it in Georgian style.

A survey of 1723 shows that the hall and Constable's Lodging were used as the governor's residence. The 'gunner' had a house (now gone) immediately north of the gatehouse. The L-shaped range in the south-east part of the castle was partly a store house and partly a 'stables formerly a barracks'. Carey's Mansion and the rooms between the hall and the curtain wall had all been demolished, presumably because this amount of accommodation was no longer needed and it was cheaper to demolish redundant buildings than to maintain them. At some point, too, the roof and floors of the gatehouse were removed. Apart from residual military use, the castle increasingly resembled a country house used intermittently as a grace-and-favour residence for the governor.

CARISBROOKE AS MONUMENT AND RESIDENCE

By the mid-19th century, even the use of the castle as the governor's residence had ceased, with the incumbents preferring to live elsewhere; the Constable's Lodging was occupied by the keeper of the castle, who was responsible for its maintenance and management. The Isle of Wight was now becoming a tourist destination, with the castle one of its principal attractions.

By this time Carisbrooke had decayed considerably, and it passed into the care of the Office of Works in 1856. The first restoration work was carried out by Philip Hardwick, a London architect, in that year. Although funds ran out before he could implement all the restorations he had planned, he converted the L-shaped building in the south-east corner of the inner bailey to its present form and refurbished the Constable's Lodging, where he restored the medieval windows on the basis of surviving evidence. He revealed William de Montacute's late 14th-century fireplace in the hall, and the earlier window behind it, as well as the remains of the chapel of St Peter. He also demolished the chapel of St Nicholas to convert it into a picturesque ruin.

Some form of military use for the castle continued into the late 19th century, as from 1853 it was the base of the Isle of Wight Artillery Militia,

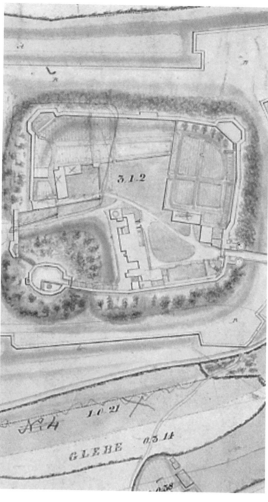

Left: A plan of the castle in 1851, which shows the layout of the governors' garden at that date (top right)
Below: The Isle of Wight Artillery Militia training at the castle in the late 19th century

who used the buildings in the south-east corner as barracks and trained on guns mounted on the north-west bastion. This corps of artillery was made up of civilian men who trained as soldiers in their spare time. By 1863 they numbered over 300. In wartime, they were called up for home defence, mainly in the coastal forts and gun batteries on the Isle of Wight, though many joined the regular army.

Towards the end of the century, Carisbrooke received renewed royal interest from Princess Beatrice, Queen Victoria's youngest daughter. When Beatrice's husband, Prince Henry of Battenberg, died of fever while returning from the Ashanti war (in what is now Ghana) in 1896, she

succeeded him as governor of the Isle of Wight. She had a long association with the island dating back to her childhood at Osborne House, and she maintained these close links until her death in 1944 (see opposite).

In 1897 the gatehouse was restored as a memorial to Prince Henry by Percy Stone, a local architect working on the island, who had published the first study of the castle's history and architecture in 1891. It became the first home of the Carisbrooke Castle Museum, which at that time focused mainly on Charles I. Stone's other major work in the castle was the restoration of the chapel of St Nicholas as a memorial to King Charles. Despite some opposition from those who wished to maintain the chapel as such, in 1919 a decision was made to transform it into a memorial to the men of the island who had died in the First World War, and Stone carried out this work too.

The great hall was re-roofed and gained its present windows in 1901, and a flat-roofed octagonal extension was added to the south of the Constable's Lodging. When Princess Beatrice decided to use the castle as her summer home from 1913, the hall and Constable's Lodging were adapted for her use: many internal fittings, such as panelling and

Princess Beatrice

Princess Beatrice (1857–1944) was the youngest daughter of Queen Victoria, and was also her mother's favourite. She spent much of her life as the queen's companion at Osborne House, thus beginning her strong associations with the Isle of Wight. The queen only allowed Beatrice to marry her fiancé, Prince Henry of Battenberg, when the couple agreed that they would continue to live at court. After their marriage in 1885 they lived at Osborne, and in 1890 apartments were provided for them above the Durbar Room there. They had four children.

Queen Victoria made Prince Henry governor of the island, and when he died in 1896 Beatrice succeeded him in this role, while remaining the queen's companion and unofficial secretary, and living at Osborne Cottage on the Osborne estate. She therefore already had strong links with Carisbrooke Castle before she took up residence there. In 1898 she opened a memorial museum to her husband in the gatehouse. Later, Beatrice supported the restoration work on the chapel of St Nicholas, giving the altar painting as a memorial to her youngest son, Maurice, who was killed at the battle of Ypres in 1914.

After the death of the last deputy governor in 1913, Princess Beatrice decided to revive the lapsed custom by which governors of the Isle of Wight took up residence in the castle, and moved in after making some alterations, such as adding a bathroom, to make it more up to date. The period that Beatrice lived at Carisbrooke is still remembered by some islanders. According to Mrs Moira Griffin, whose father, Jack Kenway White, worked as a footman to the princess in the 1930s:

'My father enjoyed his time working for her in the palaces in London, and he used to tell me about all the kings he had met. At the castle he lived in the building across the courtyard from the well house, which was connected to the princess's house by an underground corridor. It was on the island that he met my mum. Princess Beatrice gave them a lovely blanket as a wedding present – I still have it – and she let them take photos of her with their box camera.'

For 25 years, until 1938, Princess Beatrice's personal standard flew over the keep when she was in residence, mainly in the summer. Princess Beatrice died at the age of 87 at her last home, Brantridge Park, Sussex, in 1944.

> The queen only allowed Beatrice to marry her fiancé, Prince Henry of Battenberg, when the couple agreed that they would continue to live at court

window seats, survive from her time. The L-shaped range in the south-east corner of the castle was adapted to provide accommodation for her staff, and a tunnel was built between it and Beatrice's apartments to allow them easy access. Landscaping, garden ornaments on the castle banks and even the seating on one of Carey's 'knights' also reflect her influence and use of the castle. After her death in 1944, the hall and Constable's Lodging became the present home of the Carisbrooke Castle Museum, managed by its trustees.

MODERN-DAY CARISBROOKE

Since then the castle has come to be viewed mainly as an ancient monument and a visitor attraction. It also remains a centre for island ceremonies and pageantry and thereby a symbol of the identity of the Isle of Wight. Most physical changes since the Second World War have been to deal with the growth and changing needs of tourism, but also to maintain and display the site. Work to recontour the bailey banks in the 1920s uncovered the wall of the Saxon enclosure, which had been buried within the massive Norman earthworks.

Alterations have included the adaptation of existing buildings as cafes and exhibition space. A particular focus has been to provide new accommodation for the donkeys in the former works yard. Most recently, the privy garden has been redesigned by former BBC *Gardener's World* presenter Chris Beardshaw, and a new ticket office has been built between the gatehouse and the Elizabethan gate on the site of the former Victorian gatekeeper's house. For the last 50 years, all these works have been preceded by archaeological investigations which have helped to reveal that the Carisbrooke hill has a long and complex history starting at least 500 years before the castle that we see today.